How to Respond to Your Culturally Diverse Student Population

Sarah LaBrec Wyman

Association for Supervision and Curriculum Development
Alexandria, Virginia

About the Author

Sarah LaBrec Wyman is a graduate of the School of Education at Boston College and is currently a reading instructor at Mesa School in Cortez, Colorado.

Association for Supervision and Curriculum Development
1250 N. Pitt Street, Alexandria, VA 22314
Telephone: (703) 549-9110. FAX: (703) 549-3891.

Printed in the United States of America.

Ronald S. Brandt, *Executive Editor*
Nancy Modrak, *Managing Editor, Books*
Jennifer Beun, *Assistant Editor*
Gary Bloom, *Manager, Design and Production Services*
Stephanie Kenworthy, *Assistant Manager, Design and Production Services*
Valerie Sprague, *Desktop Publisher*

ASCD Stock No.: 611-93180
Price: $6.95
ISBN: 0-87120-226-3

Library of Congress Cataloging-in-Publication Data

Wyman, Sarah LaBrec.
　How to respond to your culturally diverse student population / Sara LaBrec Wyman.
　　p.　cm.
　Includes bibliographical references.
　ISBN 0-87120-226-3
　1. Minorities—Education—United States.　2. Minorities—Education—United States—Curricula.　3. Multicultural education—United States—Curricula.　4. Discrimination in education—United States.　5. Educational equalization—United States.
LC3731.W96　　1993　　　　　　　　　　　　　93-39420
371.97'0973—dc20　　　　　　　　　　　　　　　CIP

How to Respond to Your Culturally Diverse Student Population

1
The Case for Multicultural Education

Causes for Concern

The disproportionate failure and dropout rates of students of color, in light of the increasing percentage of such students in the U.S. population, presents a challenge to teachers, administrators, and our entire educational system. In the mid-1980s, 16 percent of white adults, 44 percent of blacks, and 56 percent of Hispanics were functionally or marginally illiterate. Forty-seven percent of black 17-year-olds were fully illiterate (Kozol 1985). Furthermore, while the current dropout rate for all students is roughly 25 percent (Wehlage 1989), nationwide 40 percent of Hispanic and 48 percent of Native-American students do not graduate from high school (Flores 1991). The proportion of students of color in American public high schools increased from 21 to 27 percent between 1970 and 1980. By 1995, 34 percent of students in American public schools will be Hispanic and nonwhite, and nearly half of all school age pupils will be from nonwhite cultural backgrounds by 2020 (Fiske 1991). These demographic changes indicate an increase in the number of students who are at risk of dropping out of school (Rumberger 1991).

The Purpose of this Book

Your school may opt to address its multicultural student body through a variety of means. I have compiled the following research literature with the hopes that you, as a teacher or administrator, may use it as a means of holistic self-examination, helping you to consider your school's responses to its culturally diverse student population. Those responses can be divided into five categories, which are the subjects of the remaining chapters in this book:

- Curriculum (Chapter 2)
- Instruction (Chapter 3)
- School policies (Chapter 4)
- Staffing (Chapter 5)
- Special encouragement (Chapter 6)

Each chapter ends with a list of questions designed to help you examine the ways your school addresses its students.

A Dilemma for Students of Color

In terms of the likelihood that they will experience success in public schools, our students of color are clearly "at risk." A variety of factors influence such a student's encounter with the public school system. Chief among these is that American schools are controlled by and reflect the dominant white culture. "The maintenance of one's community, history, language, talents, and skills is of paramount importance to any group of people. Yet for people of color, efforts in those areas are consistently and systematically threatened by current school practice" (Hidalgo, McDowell, and Siddle 1990, p. 135). The dominant group thus determines how minority education is structured and how minorities are treated in school (Ogbu 1988). Because their home culture can be at odds with that of the school, students of color are often left feeling "torn between two worlds," a dilemma noted by several researchers (Fordham 1990, Fordham and Ogbu 1986, Koerner 1992, Weis 1985). Often, these students find ways to camouflage their successful academic efforts to maintain acceptance by their peers (Ogbu 1988). Students of dominated groups appear to use two other coping strategies in dominant group controlled schools.

First, nonwhite students survive public education by participating in a "resistance culture," a lived cultural pattern that has been documented by numerous researchers. Ogbu (1988) writes of the distinct black cultural frame of reference that affects blacks' relationship with institutions dominated by whites. Because subordinate groups do not want to act like the dominant or exploiting group, they are often ambivalent or oppositional. He notes a paradox in that blacks say they desire education and realize that it provides a way out of poverty, but behave in a counterproductive manner by being tardy, not completing homework, and not taking school seriously. Creating a counterculture via dress, mannerisms, speech, and other behaviors is a way for students of color to distance themselves from the dominant culture and at the same time challenge the authority of the school. Stanlaw and Peshkin (1988) believe the dialect and distinct language forms used by blacks today are a symbol of separatism, promoting black solidarity and identity while at the same time excluding the majority.

This differentiation hurts students of color academically, which, in turn, limits their future employment opportunities. Black students may say they are committed to education, but as they grow older and assess the realities, they become disillusioned by what they see (Ogbu 1988). If a student perceives a lack of access to economic opportunities because parents and adults in his community are not working, high school graduation holds little promise for the future (Wehlage 1989). The result is "leveled aspirations" (MacLeod 1987) and, perhaps, participation in a resistance culture that fulfills immediate needs.

As a second coping strategy, students of dominated groups often suppress their cultural heritage and become "raceless." Unfortunately, the characteristics that lead to success in school (doing one's homework, arriving on time, speaking standard English, striving for good grades) are considered "white" behaviors. Blacks can be successful in white-controlled schools, but to succeed in this white academic realm, they must often relinquish their cultural frame of identity and "act white." Many blacks feel this is betrayal (Ogbu 1988).

> The burden rests upon people of color to disassociate themselves from their beliefs and assume the others' culture and behavior. If we hesitate or resist, the U.S.

educational system applies ready labels to categorize and sort us into lower tracks and lower expectations (Hidalgo et al. 1990, p. 137).

Rather than forcing such a choice on students of subordinated populations, we should attempt to make public education a positive experience for all students. This necessitates recognition of culturally diverse student populations, because the numerous and various blatant and subtle effects of public education controlled by the dominant culture can result in a student of color feeling that education is not for her.

Public Schools, Power, and Prejudice

Neo-Marxists accuse schools of merely reproducing the class structure and social relationships necessary to maintain capitalist profits and capitalist division of labor (Bowles and Gintis 1976), adversely affecting minorities who are disproportionately represented among the lower classes. Apple (1990) and Giroux (1988) write of how schools replicate the economic structure and status quo by contributing to the maintenance of inequality found in race, class, and gender. Ogbu attributes the academic success or failure of students of color to their economic and social status, and Banks (1981) states that schools have been reflections of society as opposed to agents of change. According to Greer (1972), many children come away from school with "a learning experience precisely appropriate to the place assigned them and their families in the social order" (p. 152).

Similarly, Cummins (1990) examines the academic problems of minority students in light of a school's ability to mirror or reverse power relations within society. Because the majority group controls the schools, it is largely responsible for the success or failure of all students. Cummins, who assesses a school's efforts in terms of the concept of empowerment, believes that whether students of color are "empowered" or "disabled" depends directly on the nature of their encounters with the education system. These encounters are influenced by the degrees to which the language and culture of nonmajority students are part of the school program, the minority community's participation in the educational system is fostered, and educators are supportive of students of color in instruction and assessment.

Overall, Cummins notes that if minority groups (1) have positive relationships with their own and the majority cultures, (2) do not view themselves as inferior, and (3) are comfortable with their own cultural values, they will not experience widespread school failure. Sleeter (1991) also writes of potential empowerment of a student through multicultural education.

Pang (1990) agrees: "For minority children, negative perceptions of their ethnic groups can evolve into self-degrading feelings, especially if these messages are reinforced in their school and society" (p. 29). She warns that educators must examine schools to become cognizant of attitudes, behaviors, situations, and expressions that reinforce prejudicial beliefs. She believes educators can guide society in ridding institutions of unintentional prejudice. Molnar (1989) points out that schools have the unique opportunity to mold children, thereby influencing our future. He believes schools can foster comprehension of the devastating affects of racism on individuals and society, and they can promote the belief that *different* does not imply *inferior.*

According to a recent survey of students, teachers, and administrators, occurrences of racism in schools across America have increased (Stover 1990). "Race prejudice in the form of ethnocentrism may act to institutionalize cultural bias," according to Gougis (1986, p. 147). Katz (1975) delineates three indications of racism that can be seen in schools:

- personal prejudices or ideologies,
- institutional practices and policies that benefit particular groups or harm others, and
- educational inequalities that vary with ethnic groups.

Prejudice of whites toward ethnic minorities in the school setting "adversely affect[s] [minority] students' daily academic performance by reducing their willingness to persist at academic tasks and interfering with the cognitive processes involved in learning" (Gougis 1986, p. 147). Other researchers have documented the effects of racist behavior on self-esteem and, therefore, academic endeavors (Murray and Clark 1990, Pollard 1989).

Potentially, schools can have a profound impact in the fight against racism by addressing the interpersonal aspects of racism, and by offering school and classroom activities that teach about oppression and recognize the strengths and contributions of various cultures (Molnar 1989). Studying, working, and interacting with students from other races decreases stereotypes (Foster 1989). Moreover, educators in all schools should be actively concerned with the impact of racism because ignoring the issue tacitly implies that it is acceptable or insignificant (Pollard 1989). Researchers differentiate between desegregation, which is aimed at removing the racial identifiability of a school by the placement of students and staff, and integration, which is "a social process involving mutual acceptance" (Donato, Menchara, and Valencia 1991, p. 55). Integration requires the support of school officials, teachers, students, and the local community. It is the standard by which schools with multicultural student populations should be measured.

Although much attention is being given to current reform movements in education, none looks promising in terms of meeting the needs of minorities and the poor (Selakovich 1984). The "crisis" reports of the 1980s go so far as to suggest that the equality movement of the 1960s and '70s—equal access—has undermined excellence (Bastian, Fruchter, Gittell, Greer, and Haskins 1986). Bastian and her co-authors deny the myth of a golden age of schooling by stating that egalitarianism in education never occurred, so it cannot be blamed for school failure. Academic excellence is a dominant theme in the 1980s reform movement, but all are not convinced that this is the correct track: "The crisis in public education has not developed because we have short-changed those at the top, but because we have grossly disserved those on the bottom" (Bastian et al. 1986, p. 27). Shor predicts the recommendations of various commission reports will bring about "the collision of Standard English with minority students," and the increase in proportions of nonwhite pupils in public schools combined with cuts in bilingual programs will perpetuate academic failure of students of color and lead to hostility (Shor 1986, p. 158).

Public Schools and Culture

Culture, which provides "a general design for living and patterns for interpreting reality," (Nobles 1990, p. 23) consists of behaviors, ideas, attitudes, habits, customs, beliefs, values, language, rituals, and ceremonies. "Current views of minority experiences, identity, and competencies . . . emphasize the increased positive potentials of flexibility and adaptability in multicultural persons, as well as the importance of developing inter-ethnic competencies" (Ramirez and Cox 1980, p. 54). Indeed, survey data taken from Mexican-American parents and community members indicate a preference for the bicultural goals of first-language maintenance and cultural identity (Ramirez and Cox 1980). All aspects of education are cultural (Nobles 1990); therefore, schools can potentially support the development of bicultural identities by students of color, and the acceptance of such individuals by the majority population.

Ogbu (1986) states that the complex and culturally pluralistic nature of American society is currently not reflected in the schools. Our schools need to "come to terms with the pluralistic reality of American society. An 'equal status pluralism' is required. . . . " (Ogbu 1986, p. 85). He believes people have the right to retain the cultures of their homes and communities as well as become knowledgeable about those of the dominant Euro-American society.

Education that recognizes and responds to the needs of your culturally diverse students can be called *multicultural* or *multi-ethnic* education. Sleeter and Grant's (1990) thorough analysis of multicultural education programs resulted in the articulation of a taxonomy that can help to define and examine the concept of multicultural education. The researchers identify five approaches to multicultural education.

- "Teaching the Culturally Different" guides students of color in their transition into the dominant culture.
- "Human Relations" fosters harmony and appreciation among students of varying cultural backgrounds.
- "Single Group Studies" exposes students to experiences, ideas, contributions, and various cultural groups through different courses.

- "Multicultural Education" changes the school program, including staffing, curriculum and instruction, to reflect the diverse cultures of populations within the school, promoting cultural pluralism and social equality.
- "Education that is Multicultural and Social Reconstructionist" educates students to take action against social structural inequality and fosters cultural pluralism.

Supporters of multicultural education base their stance on principles of democracy, egalitarianism, and pluralism (Pang 1990). According to Banks (1981), as a result of multi-ethnic education, students should gain knowledge, skills, and attitudes that enable them to function productively within their ethnic culture, the mainstream culture, and across other ethnic cultures. Prejudice should be reduced, and students should not feel the need to deny their ethnic heritage in order to succeed in school and society in general.

Historically, schools justified erasing ethnicity with the belief that people of color would encounter more difficulties if they attempted to retain ethnicity while striving for success in mainstream American society. "Hence, cultural domination in the guise of acculturation and assimilation has been the modus operandi for American education and curriculum development" (Nobles 1990, p. 6). Students from nonwhite cultural backgrounds were basically required to deny their cultural identity (Kaestle 1983). Indeed, many educators fostered the feeling of shame at being foreign (Tyack 1974).

Americans were threatened by potential separatist movements and conflicts caused by dual identity. Early social scientist models of personality conflict and cultural replacement concluded that problems resulted from cultural diversity and thus supported assimilation (Ramirez and Cox 1980).

> Throughout much of our history, active identification with an ethnic group has been viewed by social scientists, educators, and politicians as dangerous. Individuals' ethnic identification and ethnic group solidarity were viewed as obstacles to the development of an 'American national character,' to national unity, and were thought to be a basis for a loose collection of diverse, separate ethnic, racial, and religious groups. One was either foreigner or American—and to become an American the

'foreigner' was required to deny his cultural identity (Ramirez and Cox 1980, p. 54).

For education to be appropriate for children of a particular cultural group, the group's culture must be understood because one's education is guided by one's culture, and all aspects of education are cultural (Nobles 1990). Researchers Cardenas and Zamora (1980) recognize the importance of the relationship between a student's culture and an education program. If the characteristics of a student of color are not compatible with those required by the educational program, "the teaching of minority children is analogous to the placement of a round peg in a square hole. Neither of the two shapes precludes the successful completion of the activity; it is the incompatibility between the two that constitutes the problem" (p. 193).

Possible relationships between ethnic groups and the dominant group are explained by various theories, which can be used to guide school policy.

Assimilation. In assimilation the minority culture conforms to the majority culture. According to Hernandez (1989), this conformity must be cultural and structural. Cultural assimilation entails taking on behavior, values, beliefs, and lifestyles of the dominant culture. Structural assimilation involves participation in the institutions and organizations of society. Simply put, the minority defers to the dominant. With assimilation as a goal, school curriculum, instruction, organization, and policy represent the single dominant culture's orientation. The experiences and cultural elements of ethnic groups are ignored as students conform. A school operating under the assimilation orientation simply continues with its programs and policies without making any special efforts on behalf of the multicultural student population, or the school attempts to foster assimilation of ethnic minority students to the values and standards of white students. As previously discussed, this forces the student of color to "act white" in order to succeed (Sagar and Schofield 1984).

Amalgamation. Also called the melting pot theory, amalgamation is another possible orientation for school policy guiding the relationship between ethnic groups and the dominant group. A new culture containing and incorporating the best from all cultures supposedly results from multicultural contact under this framework. With amalgamation, all involved groups give up some aspects of their culture and gain others. A school's role would be to teach in ways that recognize the contributions of all cultures (Hernandez 1989).

Cultural pluralism. Sometimes referred to as "tossed salad," cultural pluralism explains the relationship between the dominant culture and other cultures. In this relationship various cultures coexist with distinct cultural identities intact. In a modified version of cultural pluralism, minority cultures adapt to the majority but retain separate identities (giving rise to the term "hyphenated Americans"). Implications for schools would include staffing that reflects the cultural diversity of the students, native language instruction, and ethnicity in the core curriculum (Hernandez 1989). A school can foster integrated pluralism by reaffirming the equality of all ethnic groups within the school. All students are exposed to various perspectives, values, and cultures, and the school actively supports positive intergroup relations and interactions (Sagar and Schofield 1984). When cultural pluralism guides school policy, students should receive a multicultural education.

Summary

School failure is more likely to be experienced by students of color than by students from the white majority. The fact that American schools are controlled by and reflect the dominant white culture must be considered when examining the relationship between students of color and public education. A student of color who feels his home culture is at odds with that of the school often adopts unsatisfactory coping strategies to stay in school, or leaves school entirely. We must counter these unacceptable alternatives by making public education a positive experience for all—thereby empowering each pupil. This necessitates

• acknowledging culturally diverse student populations,

- conceding the potential role public schools play in preserving status quo power relations and perpetuating prejudice in society, and
- recognizing the nature of the relationship between schools and culture.

Education that acknowledges and responds to the various needs of our culturally diverse students—multicultural education—may then be attempted. As a result of this multicultural education, all students will leave our schools with the knowledge, skills, and attitudes that enable them to function productively within their individual culture, the mainstream culture, and across cultures (Banks 1981).

2
Curriculum

CURRICULUM CAN BE DEFINED AS A COURSE OF STUDY THAT GUIDES how knowledge is conveyed and encourages the aspiration to know and the "internalization of behavior and/or attitudes consistent with the knowledge learned" (Nobles 1990, p. 10). Clearly, if the curriculum is dominated by the culture of the white majority, students perceive that the behaviors, ideas, customs, and values of others are illegitimate or unimportant. Nobles notes the need for a core curriculum for all that addresses various cultural differences. "In effect, we need to work toward a monoliterate society by utilizing multicultural processes and methods" (p. 20). The curriculum should surround a core body of knowledge that takes into account the cultural realities of the students in your school.

Others agree that the cultural backgrounds of students in the school must be reflected in the curriculum (Asante 1991, Banks 1981, Gay 1990, Nobles 1990, Office of Minority Affairs 1988). Reform in school curriculum has been mandated by the legal and moral tenants of desegregation in order to equalize educational opportunities for all students (Gay 1990). The teaching of basic skills must be unhooked from "the cultural chauvinism and psychological hegemony that prevails in the schools" according to Ogbu (1986, p. 84). In addition to being an agent of cultural bias (Gougis 1986) and a perpetuator of racism (Murray and Clark 1990), the current ethnocentric or Eurocentric curriculum is academically lacking as it is limited in facts by its perspective (Asante 1991; Hilliard, Payton-Stewart, and Williams 1990). The curriculum of your school should reflect the diversity of your school's population, whether it includes African Americans, Native Americans, Chicanos, or one of the many other ethnic and cultural groups.

Multiculturalists who specifically support the infusion of African content into the curriculum are called Afrocentrists. Afrocentrism proponent Molefi Kete Asante (1991) states that Afrocentrism means viewing the child of African descent as a subject of history. He also writes of the need to center all children "within the context of familiar cultural and social references from their own historical settings" (p. 28). Asante's scholarship on the situation of African-American students can also be applied to other students of color. He claims that by ignoring the historical contributions of African Americans, we devalue their culture. Non-Anglo students experience "cultural dislocation" when they attend school. Leaving out contributions of nonwhites de-centers students of color and, moreover, misinforms all of your students. According to Asante, artificial multicultural education maintains European homogeneity and fits "others" in as segments. True multicultural education results from pluralism without hierarchy. Cultural grounding your students will lead to empowerment (Asante 1991).

In the introduction to their book about infusing African and African-American content into the school curriculum, Hilliard and others (1990) state that the goal of this infusion is to present a more complete truth about the human experience, as opposed to the Eurocentric view that dominates public schools. The first National Conference of the Infusion of African and African-American Content in the School Curriculum identified generic goals for the process of infusing multicultural content into a traditional, Eurocentric curriculum:

1. The general history of the cultural group must be understood so that students can answer the questions *Who in the world am I?* and *How in the world did I get here?*

2. Teachers must proficiently grasp the histories of the nonmajority group or groups to decide how to best use curriculum materials.

3. Curriculum materials must be developed for all disciplines so that students can acquire an interdisciplinary understanding of the diverse groups.

4. Schools must acquire curriculum materials such as books, videotapes, maps, artifacts, and films that support curriculum infusion.

5. Community members must be made aware of the curriculum infusion endeavors and their participation

encouraged. Students and community members can create curriculum resources.

6. For curricular change to be lasting, the Conference notes that changes in the structure of the school and training of the staff are necessary (Hilliard et al. 1990).

In his research, Banks (1981) warns against counterproductive assumptions and approaches to the teaching of ethnic studies. First, ethnic studies conceptualized as ethnic minority studies focus on non-white minority groups. Some educators view ethnic studies as being exclusively for ethnic minorities as opposed to all students. Others think of a multicultural program as additions of isolated facts to the main curriculum, or as the study of strange and exotic customs and holidays. These conceptions of ethnic studies are superficial, and should be avoided. Other researchers agree that a school's cultural pluralism should be incorporated into the total curriculum and not merely acknowledged in special add-on ways, such as sprinkling cultural heroes, music, and food into the school environment (Asante 1991, Nobles 1990, Pine and Hilliard 1990, Pollard 1989).

In 1989 Hirsch published a list of what the culturally literate American needs to know. His work has been criticized as Eurocentric, elitist, and neglectful of the contributions and accomplishments of people of color. Pearl (1991) points out that Hirsch's list includes the word "Chicano," but only one person of Mexican-American heritage—Joan Baez—is mentioned. This is an example of how people of color are devalued by the dominant group in society. Pearl maintains that the lack of Chicano content in school curriculum contributes to Chicano school failure. In 1972, only 7 percent of the secondary schools in the Southwest offered Chicano history as part of the curriculum. Researcher Valencia (1991) also believes that the inclusion of Chicano cultural components in instruction would aid in reducing Chicano school failure.

The Search for Truth

Hilliard and others (1990) write that the search for truth should be the paramount goal for pupils. The curriculum must thus be grounded in valid scholarship, necessitating a re-examination of our history curriculum, among others. Such an endeavor will reveal that myth is often taught as fact; history texts are full of examples of distorted Eurocentric or Anglocentric perspectives (Hilliard et al. 1990).

A revolution in teaching history and social studies has been smoldering in many states for years (Reinhold 1991). The New York State education department helped bring the multicultural curriculum controversy to the public's attention when a 1990 a task force report entitled "A Curriculum of Inclusion" accused the New York social studies curriculum of encouraging "white nationalism" and ethnocentrism. The committee's recommendations for a social studies curriculum, "One Nation, Many Peoples: A Declaration of Interdependence," states:

> The time has come to *recognize cultural interdependence.* We propose that the principle of respect for diverse cultures is critical to our nation, and we affirm that a right to cultural diversity exists. We believe that the schoolroom is one of the places where this cultural *interdependence* must be reflected (New York State Social Studies Review and Development Committee 1991, pp. xi–xii).

A similar revolution in teaching history and social studies has occurred in California (Reinhold 1991).

An analogous re-examination of curriculum can be seen in English. Rather than continue with the static track of the sacred literary canon supported by such educators as Bloom, Hirsch, and Ravich, the National Council of Teachers of English Assembly on Literature for Adolescents recommends tuning into the "diverse voice of America" (Charles 1991). The Council declares:

> We acknowledge the existence, legitimacy and art of all the diverse American literatures, including those written by members of racial and ethnic minority groups, literatures which have been excluded from the canon. We are not threatened by, nor are any of our standards lowered by, this inclusion. Rather, we are strengthened by it. We are tuned to the multicultural reality of America (Charles 1991, p. 4).

Dewitt (1991) agrees, stating that a school's English program must include literature that reflects the cultural diversity of its student population, while at the same time meets intellectual, moral, and civic missions and goals.

Similarly, Stover (1991) gives four reasons why the literature program in any school should reflect cultural diversity:

1. All students need some personal connection with the literature they read in order to view it as relevant. Traditionally, English department offerings are Eurocentric, ignoring minority student cultures.

2. All students should be exposed to alternative perspectives and values to function comfortably in America's increasingly culturally diverse society. Students need to examine their own and other's values.

3. A literature program should reflect cultural diversity to aid students in understanding connections between art and culture.

4. Numerous and various literature sources are readily available for making English curriculum appropriate for a culturally diverse student population.

Limiting the English curriculum to Eurocentric literature not only limits perspectives, it can also perpetuate prejudice. On the other hand, an extensive study revealed that the exposure of white students to the life histories of famous black Americans, realistic fiction that portrayed blacks positively in multi-racial situations, and various multicultural materials, resulted in a significant decrease in racial prejudice (Lynch 1987).

Similarly, Charles (1991) suggests teaching Native-American literature to fight the perpetuation of stereotypes. The National Council of Teachers of English (NCTE) suggests that English teachers in schools with Native-American students present oral (traditional) and written (contemporary) Native-American literature. The NCTE further suggests that teachers select examples from diverse Native-American tribes throughout the United States. "Language and literature are important factors in the maintenance of Native American identity" (Charles 1991, p. 4). Moreover, Native-American literature provides both universal themes and cultural specific themes, and shows all students that Native Americans present their views intelligently and eloquently.

Furthermore, the inclusion of literature representative of the cultural diversity of the school community is necessary in light of the increasing number of students of color and the relative shortage of minority teachers. A school's efforts at changing the English curriculum to include non-white literature are indicative of the school's values (Stover 1991). Though shortages may limit whom you hire, you can show respect for diversity "as at least one small step toward building a future citizenry that understands the diversity of the American society and that validates the experiences of all our young adults" (Stover 1991, p. 14).

Questions for Self-Evaluation

1. Is multicultural education a part of my school's curriculum goals?
2. How are people of color portrayed in my school's curriculum?
3. Are the histories, perspectives, and contributions of people of color included in my curriculum?
4. How are curriculum decisions made?
5. Have all disciplines developed curriculum materials incorporating the histories, perspectives, and contributions of people of color so that an interdisciplinary understanding of all groups is promoted?
6. Does the library include books by and about people of color?
7. Are available media materials representative of the cultural diversity of my school?
8. Are teachers and students aware of available multicultural library and media materials?
9. How are books and materials acquired?

How to Get Started

- Develop a curriculum, grounded in solid scholarship, that reflects the diversity of your school's population.

- Train teachers so that they are sufficiently knowledgeable about the various groups to decide how to best use curriculum materials.
- Develop curriculum materials for all disciplines that enable students to acquire an interdisciplinary understanding of the diverse groups.
- Acquire materials such as books, videotapes, maps, artifacts, and films that support a multicultural curriculum.
- Inform community members of curriculum infusion endeavors and encourage their participation.

3
Instruction

IN ADDITION TO MAKING CHANGES IN CURRICULUM, YOUR SCHOOL
may address the needs of its culturally diverse student
population through specific measures related to
instruction. Overall, teachers must strive to interact with
all cultures in the classroom in the content, style,
language, approaches and motivations, assessment and
reward methods of their instruction (Lynch 1987).
Research data show that "cultural patterns influence the
way information is perceived, organized, processed, and
utilized" (Hilliard in Hale-Benson 1986, p. xxiii); yet school
culture is usually consistent with the values, behaviors,
learning styles, and expectations of the Anglo home (Banks
1981).

Banks (1981) therefore recommends that local ethnic
learning styles be reflected in curriculum and instruction.
Weis (1988) states that researchers with a cultural
perspective suggest that, rather than changing students
and parents, school personnel should learn to value the
culture of origin and accommodate culturally specific
learning strategies that students of non-majority cultures
have required. Cross-cultural research supports the belief
that competencies are learned within the context of certain
cultural tasks, activities, and interpersonal contacts.
Culture, therefore, affects cognition by dictating which
types of experiences a student undergoes. The cultural
experiences a student has had will affect his efforts to
understand the meaning of a task presented to him (Miller-
Jones 1989).

A poem by an Apache child in Arizona cited in Cazden
(1988, p. 67) addresses the mismatching that students of
color often experience in their education:

Have you ever hurt about baskets?
I have, seeing my grandmother weaving for a long time.
Have you ever hurt about work?
I have, because my father works too hard and tells how
    he works.
Have you ever hurt about cattle?
I have, because my grandfather has been working on
    cattle for a long time.
Have you ever hurt about school?
I have, because I learned a lot of words from school,
And they are not my words.

Cazden believes the appropriate response to those who "hurt about school" is to find ways to make connections between the words and meanings of nonmajority children and the majority, thereby avoiding "cultural discontinuity." This discontinuity, also called "sociolinguistic interference," can occur when the discourse patterns of one's home environment are different from those in the school setting (Cazden 1988).

An example of a school response to such discontinuity, which worked with Hawaii's indigenous Polynesian descent minority students, would be to modify lesson structures. In this case, Hawaiian minority students were permitted to verbally participate without being called on by the teacher; choral-type responses are a cultural discussion style for these students. This instructional change resulted in an improvement in the reading and verbal skills of the students (Cazden 1988).

In order to avoid misinterpretations, teachers and administrators must understand how non-Anglo beliefs translate into the demeanor and conduct of students of color (Locust 1990). Philips (1983) explains a relative lack of Native-American verbal participation in the classroom as resulting from the absence of social conditions that they have learned as necessary preconditions for their verbal participation. The Native-American students of Warm Springs were less willing to act when the teacher required them to speak alone in front of other students, and when the teacher dictated when the speaking must occur. Indeed, in her description of her reactions to her first college class, a Navajo student who grew up on a reservation identifies cultural differences and how they could be a problem if the instructor is unaware of Native-American society characteristics:

One after the other, the whites would talk, arguing, discussing pros and cons. In our high school we never did that. In my traditional family we did not talk unless we had to. Silence was a sign of respect for our elders. We're supposed to think about what we say before we say it. . . .We're expected to listen more than to talk or participate (Koerner 1992, p. 18).

Obviously, such beliefs could pose problems for students who are graded on class participation.

Another example of how cultural incompatibilities can lead to misjudgments can be seen in a letter written by a Native-American father to his son's teacher. Regarding his son, the father writes:

He is not culturally 'disadvantaged' but he is culturally different! . . . He is caught between two worlds, torn by two distinct cultural systems. . . . I want my child to succeed in school and in life. I don't want him to be a dropout or juvenile delinquent or to end up on drugs or alcohol because of discrimination. I want him to be proud of his rich heritage and culture, and I would like him to develop the necessary capabilities to adapt to, and succeed in, both cultures. But I need your help. What you say and what you do in the classroom, what you teach and how you teach it, and what you don't say and don't teach will have a significant effect on the potential success or failure of my child. . . . All I ask is that you work with me, not against me, to help educate my child in the best way. My son, Wind-Wolf, is not an empty glass coming into your class to be filled. He is a full basket coming into a different environment and society with something special to share. Please let him share his knowledge, heritage, and culture with you and his peers (Lake 1990, p. 51–52).

Teacher attitudes, expectations, and perceptions have a strong influence on a student's attitude toward school, his confidence, self-perceptions, and behavior. Ogbu (1986) cites poor teacher attitudes and expectations of students of color as ways education is "inferiorating." Gay (1990) found that teacher expectations are the lowest for females, poorer students, and students of color, unless those students are Asian Americans. Moreover, Payne (1989) finds that well-intentioned majority teachers are often unknowingly biased. Solomon's (1989) study of black students found that it is imperative that school personnel raise their academic expectations and encouragement of black pupils, or they will continue to fulfill the stereotype of excelling in athletics but underachieving in academics. Banks (1981) reports that teachers need positive attitudes and high academic expectations for all minority students.

Teacher-Student Interactions

Closely related to teacher attitudes and expectations are teacher-student classroom interactions. Research indicates that certain teacher behaviors, such as praise of students and acceptance of their ideas, are positively related to student achievement (Rosenshine 1971). Ogbu (1988) cites classroom interactions that favor the child of the dominant culture as one way our schools hurt students of color. Lynch (1987) charges teachers with the responsibility of making certain that

> ... neither they, nor pupils, nor the schools are discriminating negatively against pupils because of their cultural and social backgrounds. Further they will need to aim to engage all cultures in the classroom in the content, style, language, approaches and motivations, assessment and reward strategies of their teaching (p. 3).

Hernandez (1989) reports that student experiences in the same classroom can vary greatly, and this is sometimes related to ethnicity. Teachers' expectations and the attention they give to students of color compared to whites varies, as does the frequency and quality of teacher-student interactions. In their studies of patterns of racism in schools, Murray and Clark (1990) believe there is bias in the rewards, praise, reinforcement, encouragement, and hints given to students. They further report inequalities in the amount of instructional time given to majority and minority students.

Valencia (1991) bluntly asserts that teachers tend to treat Chicano students less favorably than white students. Pearl (1991) concurs in his examination of the relationship between Chicano school failure and unequal encouragement. Researcher Ortiz (1988) found that Hispanic students were not called on as often and were left out and made to share materials more often than their white peers. A high school teacher in Texas, Flores (1991) claims that whether or not Hispanic students participate often "depends entirely upon the teacher" (p. 58). He recommends that teachers believe in their students, challenge them academically, learn to pronounce their names correctly in order to show respect, and encourage them to reach out to other students. A report by the U.S. Commission on Civil Rights (1973) concludes that the quality and quantity of teacher-student interactions varied with a student's ethnic background. The report found that Chicano students received less praise and encouragement from their teachers as compared to their white peers. It also concluded that teachers criticized Chicanos more and asked them fewer probing questions.

Researchers Jackson and Cosca (1974) looked for disparities in teacher-student interaction due to ethnicity. Their study examined how teacher behaviors affected the quality of educational opportunity for students of various ethnic groups in the Southwest. Teacher verbal behaviors were coded and classroom interactions were observed. Their research identified statistically significant differences in teacher interaction with Mexican-American and Anglo students. Specifically, the study found differences in the ways teachers interact with students in five teacher behavior categories: teacher praising or encouraging students, teacher accepting or using student ideas, teacher questioning, teacher giving positive feedback, and all noncriticizing teacher talk. Anglo students were praised or encouraged 35 percent more, their ideas were used 40 percent more often, and they were questioned 21 percent more often than the Mexican-American students. Moreover, the researchers believed the study underestimated these disparities because the teachers were aware that the observers were from a Federal Civil Rights agency, and the study did not include schools currently under investigation for Civil Rights violations. The authors concluded by stating that the behaviors of teachers in the Southwest are "at least partly contributing to the poor academic achievement of many Chicano students" (p. 227).

Inservice

Closely related to the needed improvement of teacher attitudes, expectations, and interactions with students of color are special training and inservice programs. These forms of staff development can help your teachers better understand culturally diverse students. Teachers can also be involved in organizing programs that support your school's multicultural objectives (Office of Minority Affairs 1988). Banks (1981) suggests that mandatory, continuing staff development programs that address multicultural education issues be part of the school program. Asante (1991) also believes that to make curriculum relevant, teachers must become educated about the cultures they see in their classrooms. Furthermore, teachers have an important role in identifying racial and cultural biases in themselves, students, and curriculum materials, and in clarifying why prejudice and racism will not be tolerated (Office of Minority Affairs 1988, Pine and Hilliard 1990, Pollard 1989). Given these diverse responsibilities, special training sessions would be a suitable means of educating your teachers and staff.

Methodology

Methodology also can be adjusted to address the needs of your multicultural student body. Legally mandated integration does not prohibit students from segregating by choice, resulting in "desegregation without integration" (Kagan 1990, p. 10). Kagan believes that cooperative learning—having students work toward educational objectives in academically and racially heterogeneous groups—fosters positive interdependence among students. Furthermore, he found that cooperative learning results in a great improvement in racial relations among students; in a study of integrated cooperative learning teams, self-segregation was basically eradicated and friendship patterns became independent of race.

In earlier research on Mexican-American children, Kagan (1977) concluded that these pupils were more concerned with cooperative motives, such as group enhancement, than were Anglo children. When given a choice of behavioral responses in a variety of situations, Mexican-American children chose cooperative motive responses as opposed to competitive motive responses more frequently than did white students. The findings of other researchers support this—for Native Americans as well (Adams 1990, Burgess 1980, Cardenas and Zamora 1980). The use of cooperative learning methods would likely have a positive impact on the academic efforts of Mexican-American and Native-American students.

Other studies support the use of intergroup contact to reduce racial prejudice. You must consider all variables, however, for such contact to truly improve intergroup relations. For example, equal status cooperative interdependence must be supported by authority figures; in other words, if only Anglo students are placed in leadership roles within groups, prejudice may be reinforced. Having the opportunity to interact with fellow students as individuals is another necessary precondition for intergroup contact to decrease racial prejudice (Lynch 1987).

Methodology must also be flexible in terms of respecting the beliefs of students. If the teacher understands the culture of the students, misinterpretations can be avoided. A teacher of Native-American students who is aware of the cultural grounding of their reluctance to speak out should develop alternatives to oral class participation. Likewise, a biology teacher who is aware of traditional Native-American taboos against mutilation of an animal's body could avoid conflict by creating options to dissection (Locust 1990). It is a basic teaching responsibility to find the means to help all students achieve.

Assessment

Assessment is a final element of instruction that may be addressed if your school is serving a culturally diverse student population. Differences in test performance may result from culturally-related differences due to cognitive processes rather than abilities (Miller-Jones 1989). Miller-Jones therefore recommends that students' repertoires of cognitive processes and the circumstances influencing their use be considered when testing the knowledge of students from various cultural backgrounds. He further suggests that a variety of tasks, measures, and materials be used in assessing the competencies of all students.

Again, teacher creativity is called for in measuring the skills and understanding of students of color in your school.

Questions for Self-Evaluation

1. Do the teachers in my school have an understanding of the cultures they see represented in their classrooms?

2. Are teachers and supervisors aware of local ethnic learning styles?

3. Are teacher expectations lower for students of color than for Anglo students?

4. Do the teachers in my school make conscious efforts to engage all students in learning activities within the classroom?

5. Do teachers make conscious efforts to give equivalent attention and encouragement to all students?

6. Does my school support staff development programs that help teachers better understand the cultures of their students?

7. Do staff development programs address multicultural education issues?

8. Are staff members helped to identify racial and cultural biases in themselves, students, and curriculum materials?

9. Do teachers use methodology that fosters integration (e.g., cooperative learning)?

10. Do instruction and methodology conflict with the cultural beliefs of any of the students in my school?

11. Do teachers use a variety tasks, measures, and materials in assessing the competencies of students?

How to Get Started

- Value, reflect, and accommodate local ethnic learning styles and strategies in curriculum and instruction.

- Train teachers to recognize and understand how non-Anglo beliefs translate into the demeanor and conduct of students of color.

- Train teachers to respect and believe in their students, to challenge them academically, to learn proper name pronunciation, and to encourage their students to reach out to others.

- Develop mandatory, continuing staff development programs that address multicultural education issues and educate teachers about the cultures they see in their classrooms.

- Foster cooperative learning in your classrooms and ensure that methodology is flexible in terms of respecting the beliefs of students.

- Consider the students' repertoires of cognitive processes and the circumstances influencing their use when testing the knowledge of students from various cultural backgrounds.

- Use a variety of tasks, measures, and materials to assess the competencies of all students.

4
School Policies

School Philosophy _____

School policies can provide a link between curriculum
and instruction and your total educational program. These
policies influence student, teacher, and staff interactions as
well as the school climate or ethos. Your school's
dedication to multicultural education can be seen in the
school philosophy, objectives, and official statements of
educational principles (Office of Minority Affairs 1988).
Cardenas and Zamora (1980) suggest schools clearly state
that all students are capable of learning and success, and
that cultural pluralism is a positive educational goal.
Others specifically suggest that schools delineate a policy
of zero tolerance of racism in any form, thereby
eliminating questions about whether or not the district
intends to address racism (Lynch 1987, Pine and Hilliard
1990, Stover 1990). Guiding principles such as those set
forth in mission statements may help establish an
ethnically tolerant ethos. In addition, educational
institutions should consider unintended messages. For
example, if all awards are given to students from one
ethnic group, procedures and criteria need to be
evaluated, and other award categories may need to be
added.

School boards also have the ability to help establish a
racially tolerant tone. Research suggests that school
boards clarify expectations regarding racism to the entire
school community (Office of Minority Affairs 1988, Pollard
1989). At the same time, consequences for offenders
should be delineated. School boards can also be a source
of positive reinforcement for those who make efforts to
decrease racism in classrooms and the school (Pollard

1989). Moreover, the ethnic composition of your school board should reflect that of the student population (Office of Minority Affairs 1988).

Standardized Testing

One of the most important school policies affecting students of color is the use of standardized testing. The major uses of standardized testing are (1) judging the effectiveness of teachers, schools, and programs, (2) sorting students for various grouping purposes, (3) guiding curriculum decisions, and (4) making retention judgments (Snyderman and Rothman 1987). According to Valencia (1991), standardized test scores are often cited to justify unequal outcomes of the schooling process. He criticizes the use of tests with questionable reliability and validity. Also, he charges that tests are misused because they often become the major factor in educational decision making. Researchers Linn and others (1982) agree, and specifically criticize this misuse of standardized tests.

Students of color score below the national average on all standardized measures of performance (Gay 1990). This obviously has grave implications for the educational futures of these pupils. For example, such testing is relied on for retention decisions, and research has shown that being held back a grade doubles the likelihood of dropping out (Mann 1989). Mercer (1977) attributes this to the fact that standardized tests assume homogeneity, and their content is Anglo culture specific. Other researchers agree that standardized tests are culturally loaded and culture biased (Ogbu 1988, Valencia 1991).

Disproportionately lower achievement of Chicanos on standardized tests is an enduring and widespread finding in Chicano schooling research, and test misuse is seen in both intelligence and competency testing. Researchers Valencia and Aburto (1991) identify several ways in which standardized testing helps frame Chicano school failure. Historically, intelligence tests have been cited as justification from channeling Chicano students into lower tracks or special education programs. Similarly, the misuse of achievement and intelligence tests causes disproportionate numbers of Native-American children to be labeled mentally retarded or learning disabled (Locust, 1990). Such results of standardized testing have lead Banks (1981) to state that "standardized intelligence testing, in the final analysis, serves to legitimize the status quo and to keep powerless ethnic groups at the lower rungs of the social ladder" (p. 190).

Historically and philosophically, minimum competency tests have been associated with movements for educational excellence (Kreitzer, Madaud, and Haney 1989). By 1980 roughly half of the states required a passing score on a minimum competency test as one requirement for receiving a high school diploma. Passing scores on such tests are also required at specific points throughout the educational program for students to progress to a higher grade. "School-based competency testing," also frequently used by schools, is the result of state legislative mandates. Such achievement tests are typically part of statewide skill evaluations in conjunction with school reform programs. The results of these tests are then made public. Minimum competency tests (MCTs) reassure the public about tough standards in education, but evaluation of the use of such tests is not funded. "Once MCT is viewed as a powerful and politically expedient symbol, whose existence alone satisfies the demand for educational rigor, it is easy to understand why questions about impact do not get raised, let alone investigated" (Kreitzer et al. 1989, p. 133).

The use of MCTs is a school policy that needs to be evaluated because the tests adversely affect most students of color. Racial minorities are over-represented in dropouts and among students who do not pass the minimum competency tests (Kreitzer et al. 1989). When retention and advancement decisions are heavily based on test results, the use of minimum competency testing can increase the likelihood of a student of color dropping out. According to Valencia and Aburto, "it is quite clear that MCT constitutes an abuse of tests with respect to a substantial number of Chicano students" (1991, p. 229).

Tracking

Such tests often play a role in decisions related to the tracking of students. In the early 1900s, standardized tests supposedly "scientifically" justified the practice of tracking by educators challenged with accommodating new populations of pupils (Oakes 1986a). And tracking in turn "helped to institutionalize beliefs about race and class differences in intellectual abilities and to erect structural obstacles to the future social, political, and economic opportunities of those who were not white and native-born" (Oakes 1986a, p. 13).

Tracking is the policy of dividing students into different groups for different achievement levels. A student follows a sequence of courses according to the track to which he has been assigned. Typically, high schools differentiate among a college bound track, a general track, and a vocational track. Successful completion of courses in basic areas such as English and math may be graduation requirements for all students, but the academic level of the course varies with the track for which that course is offered.

Student background characteristics are strongly related to their track placement. Minority students are over-represented in the low-ability tracks and under-represented in programs for the gifted and talented (Gay 1990, Oakes 1986a). For students of color, tracking is thus a block in the path of achievement; it fosters the continuity of social class status quo, because once placed in a lower track, a student rarely has the opportunity to advance (Oakes 1986a). Course choice has been found to be the strongest school-related predictor of achievement for all students (Oakes 1988). A school's efforts at providing different educational experiences to students through tracking combined with home disadvantages "may actually limit students' opportunities to learn and contribute to lower outcomes" (Oakes 1988, p. 119). Bastian and others (1986) actually state that entitlement programs, which lead to segregated special needs classes, usually lead to more "tracking, labeling, and lowered expectations" (p. 45).

In 1972, the enrollment rate for whites in academic high school programs was 49 percent, compared with 26.8 percent for blacks and 25.2 percent for Hispanics. Little improvement for students of color was seen in 1980 when 25.5 percent of Hispanic students were taking academic track courses compared with 32.3 percent for black high school students and 41.8 percent for whites. Blacks and

Hispanics are still over-represented in vocational tracks (Baratz 1986).

Sleeter and Grant (1990) feel that a school cannot claim to provide a multicultural education program if students of color are disproportionately represented in lower track classes and among dropouts. Gay (1990) similarly believes that discrimination in the form of curriculum segregation occurs when course assignments, books and content, instructional methodologies, and materials vary according to a student's cultural background. Oakes (1988) agrees: "the distribution of actual classroom experiences, resources, and opportunities to students with different race, class, and ability characteristics may be an important schooling contribution to unequal outcomes" (p. 117).

Education reports of the 1980s indicate a shift in general goals from equality to excellence orientations. Oakes (1986a) claims that tracking in secondary schools inhibits the progression of either. In terms of instructional time and teaching quality, the opportunities to learn are fewer for students in lower tracks. The classroom climate of lower track classes is less academic and positive than that of higher academic track classes. Typical lower track class goals such as "following directions," "respecting teacher authority," "punctuality," and "learning to take a direct order" bring to mind the supposedly outdated factory model orientation of public schools of the past (Bowles and Gintis 1976, Fiske 1991). The majority of research material on tracking refutes the pedagogical premise of the policy by indicating that most students can learn as well in heterogeneous groups, and that the average or below average student's academic achievement is often higher in a heterogeneous classroom. Furthermore, positive effects of heterogeneous grouping are not limited to academics; peer relationships are more friendly in nontracked schools (Kagan 1990, Oakes 1986b). In tracked schools, on the other hand, because certain groups of students are together for much of the school day, a hierarchy exists that leads to separation and stereotyping, and affects how students perceive and are perceived by the school (Oakes 1986a).

A low score on a standardized test is not the only way students of color make it to the lower track classes. Teachers are supposed to refer students to special education based on the student's competence. Research has shown that factors other than ability, including race and cultural characteristics, play a role in referrals. Students of color, therefore, bear a risk of being inappropriately referred (Rueda 1991).

Discipline and Rules

Bias in discipline has also been identified as a pattern of racism in schools (Murray and Clark 1990). Experiences with a school's attendance and suspension policies may contribute to a student's believing that staying in school is not an option. School policies often are factors that lead to the "push out" of students (Wehlage 1989). Data indicate that school characteristics related to discipline influence the tendency to drop out (Wehlage and Rutter 1987). Not only are students of color more frequently found in lower tracks and special education classes, they are also more likely to be referred for disciplinary problems than are white students (Gay 1990). Flexibility and understanding on the part of our schools could avoid undue punishment.

Locust (1990) cites specific examples of how a school's rules and policies may have an adverse impact on Native-American students. First, a school may require a doctor's note for absences, but a physician who is not a Native American might not recognize "spiritual unwellness," which in Native-American culture is a legitimate illness. Similarly, a Native-American student may be required to stay home to help an unwell relative because group efforts are deemed important to a tribe, clan, or family. A school with Native-American students may need to excuse these non-Anglo absences without penalty to the student. Likewise, Native Americans may consider it sacrilegious to change or shower in front of other students. This may result in their failing a physical education course because their need for privacy is not accommodated. School calendars are also a potential source of penalty for Native-American students because they may not be allowed to partake in tribal ceremonies. An obvious recommendation is that schools review their policies and rules to be sure they are unbiased (Cardenas and Zamora 1980).

Questions for Self-Evaluation

1. Does my school have philosophy and mission statements that refer to cultural pluralism as an educational goal?

2. Does my school have official policies stating that racism will not be tolerated?

3. Are consequences for those guilty of racism clearly delineated?

4. Does my school board support racial tolerance?

5. Are students from a variety of ethnic groups in my school recognized with awards and honors?

6. Does the ethnic composition of the school board reflect that of my school's student population?

7. Does my school use standardized testing to judge or sort students?

8. How does standardized testing effect students of color in my school?

9. Does my school have a tracking policy?

10. How does tracking effect students of color in my school?

11. Are students of color more frequently referred for disciplinary problems than Anglo students?

12. Do my school's rules and policies accommodate the cultures of the students?

13. Do school calendars accommodate cultural differences?

How to Get Started

- Develop a school philosophy that clearly states that all students are capable of learning and success, and that cultural pluralism is a positive educational goal.

- Clarify expectations regarding racism to the entire school community, delineate consequences for offenders, and provide positive reinforcement for those who make efforts to decrease racism in classrooms and the school.

- Evaluate the uses and consequences of minimum competency tests and tracking.
- Review policies and rules to be sure they are unbiased.

5
Staffing

STATISTICS DELINEATING TRENDS IN THE TEACHING FORCE, COMBINED with those describing the changing composition of the student population, depict a disturbing picture.

> The distance between who teaches and who is taught in public schools is growing as the American pool of teachers becomes more middle-class and Anglo and as the student population embraces increasing proportions of children of color and the poor (Gay 1990).

The cultural composition of your teaching staff should reflect that of the students (Banks 1981, Cardenas and Zamora 1980, Office of Minority Affairs 1988).

In addition, you should consider the composition of administrators, counselors, media personnel, health service workers, specialists and consultants, food service workers, secretaries, clerks, custodial employees, and paraprofessionals (Office of Minority Affairs 1988).

Demographic Trends

Nationally, only 6.9 percent of the teaching force is black. This figure, which represents a sharp decrease from 18 percent two decades ago, is predicted to drop to 5 percent by 1995. Similarly, only 1.9 percent of teachers in the United States are Hispanic. In a typical teacher education department of 400 students, 362 are white, 22 black, 7 Hispanic, 3 Asian, and 2 Native American (Haberman 1989). The percentage of Chicano public school teachers continues to decrease (Valencia 1991). These statistics, combined with those describing the changing composition of the student population, indicate that we face "a future in which both white and minority children are confronted with almost exclusively white authority figures in the school" (Carnegie Task Force 1986, p. 32). School staff in general, and teachers in particular, should reflect the cultural pluralism of society for pedagogical and ethical reasons.

In addition to the Carnegie Task Force, the Holmes Group and National Education Association (NEA) have recognized the significance of the demographic trends of the nation's student population in light of the decreasing pool of teachers of color. A resolution passed by the NEA's board of directors stated:

> The NEA believes that multiracial teaching staffs are essential to the operation of nonsegregated schools. The Association deplores the current trend of diminishing numbers of minority educators. The Association urges local and state affiliates and appropriate governing bodies and agencies to work to increase the number of minority teachers and administrators to a percentage at least equal to, but not limited to, the percentage of the minority in the general population (Futrell and Robinson 1986).

One of the six goals of the Quality Education for Minorities Project, a comprehensive voice for Alaska Natives, Native Americans, black Americans, Mexican Americans, and Puerto Ricans, is to "strengthen and increase the number of teachers of minority students" (Quality Education for Minorities Project 1990).

Pedagogical Premises

The call to more closely match the proportion of minority teachers with that of minority students is pedagogically based.

> Given historical inequities in educational opportunities afforded black students, representativeness on school faculties is crucial because black teachers improve the quality of education provided to black students (Stewart 1989, p. 140).

Research indicates that the teacher's role in the lives of minority students is greater than for middle-class white students (Irvine 1988). Low-income and minority children are more teacher-dependent than are their white peers. A minority student's self-concept, therefore, is greatly influenced by his perception of his teacher's view of him. White teachers have lower expectations for black students than for whites; black students also receive less attention, encouragement, and praise from white teachers than do their white peers (Irvine 1988). Indeed, according to one study, black pupils receive two and a half times more negative feedback from white teachers than from black teachers (Aaron and Powell 1982). Also, numerous studies indicate that white teachers have more negative attitudes and beliefs about the personality traits, abilities, behaviors, and potentials of black children than do black teachers (Irvine 1988).

Failure to hire racial minority teachers and other school personnel at all levels has been identified as a pattern of racism common in schools (Murray and Clark 1990). A study of 173 large urban school districts reported that as the proportion of black teachers in a district increases, the proportion of black students referred to special education classes, suspended, or expelled decreases. Similarly, blacks are half as likely as whites to be placed in gifted programs (Farrell 1990). Simply planting black teachers in front of black students is an inappropriate response to these disturbing research results, however. Clearly, the biased behavior of white teachers needs to be addressed for the good of all students. Nevertheless, these findings justify efforts to increase the supply of teachers of color.

Misunderstandings or misinterpretations due to cultural differences between your students and teachers could be avoided by increasing the number of teachers of color on your staff. For instance, a teacher may judge a child as disobedient when the real problem lies in communication; an Anglo teacher's direct command given in the form of an indirect statement may be misinterpreted by a student of color. Delpit (1990) cites examples of students of color misbehaving in a classroom because their culture teaches them to recognize and respond to authority that is earned by the teacher through his actions, not due to him because of his role. According to Delpit (1990), "there are different attitudes in different cultural groups about which characteristics make for a good teacher. Thus, it is impossible to create a model for the good teacher without taking issues of culture and community context into account" (p. 95).

Another pedagogical premise for placing black teachers in classes with black pupils is that these pupils "lack adequate access and exposure to role models" (Thomas 1987, p. 275). Black teachers are important as role models as well as surrogate parent figures, counselors, and disciplinarians for many black children (Adair 1984, Martinez 1977). Chicano teachers are also needed as role models for Chicano and other students. Valencia (1991) believes these teachers will promote respect for ethnicity among all students. Non-black children, likewise, benefit from witnessing black adults acting as successful and responsible members of society (Graham 1987). Having the proportion of minority teachers representative of the racial balance in society is a positive experience for all:

> White students need black teachers as role models so that they can gain accurate perceptions of our multiethnic society. In addition, the presence of Black teachers in schools helps counter negative stereotypes that white children have about black people—stereotypes perpetuated by ignorance, prejudice, isolation, and distortion in the media (Irvine 1988, p. 506).

Raths (1989) analyzes the suggestions of reformers regarding the teaching force. He believes the empirical support for the argument that black teachers are best suited to teach black students is "fragile." However, he thinks that the argument has merit on the grounds of justice in that society's institutions should be open to all. Pine and Hilliard (1990) believe that a culturally diverse teaching staff is an equity message for all students. They observe that such a staff is also good for majority teachers because when the number of minority teachers is small, majority teachers interpret the actions of minority teachers through ethnic stereotypes rather than individual differences. Also, majority members often assume that the teachers who benefit from affirmative action are less competent (Pine and Hilliard 1990). Integration is fostered by the presence of a multiracial staff because such a staff counters stereotypes of racial incompetence and inferiority (U.S. Commission on Civil Rights 1976). Other researchers agree:

> The public schools educate and socialize the nation's children. Schools form children's opinions about the

larger society and their own futures. The race and background of their teachers tell them something about power and authority in contemporary America. These messages influence children's attitudes toward school, their academic accomplishments, and their views of their own and others' intrinsic worth. The views they form in school about justice and fairness also influence their future citizenship (Carnegie Task Force 1986, p. 79).

In a just society, all occupations should represent the composition of the society as a whole. For teaching, this is especially important as children's first experiences of the world outside their homes take place in elementary and secondary schools, where they learn their initial, and most long lasting social lessons (Darling-Hammond and Pittman 1987, p. 1).

Of course, the number of applicants limits your school's ability to hire teachers of color. Public schools cannot recruit and hire teachers of color if there are no qualified applicants. Thus, in spite of the fact that research recommends that school staffing correlate with the cultural composition of the students, sometimes the issue may be out of a public high school's control.

Questions for Self-Evaluation

1. Does the staff of my school reflect the cultural diversity of the student population?

2. Are certain positions identified with certain cultures?

3. Does my school recruit staff members from all cultures?

4. Does my school encourage students of color to enter the teaching profession?

How to Get Started

- Attempt to create a teaching staff whose cultural diversity reflects that of the student population for pedagogical and ethical reasons.

- Consider the cultural composition of administrators, counselors, media personnel, health service workers, specialists and consultants, food service workers, secretaries, clerks, custodial employees, and paraprofessionals.

6
Special Encouragement

YOUR SCHOOL MAY OPT TO RESPOND TO ITS CULTURALLY DIVERSE student population through special encouragement or efforts on behalf of students of color (Office of Minority Affairs 1988). To determine the appropriate educational programs for students of color, teachers of color, parents, and members of the community must contribute information regarding the kind of instruction they desire for their children (Banks 1981, Cardenas and Zamora 1980, Delpit 1990). A school's attempts to involve minority parents may foster success for nonwhite students (Davis 1986, Schierbeck 1981).

Parent Teacher Associations (PTAs) are a potential source of encouragement for students of color. They can aid in promoting acceptance and appreciation of cultural differences (Jor'dan 1990) if their members reflect the cultural diversity of the student population. Your school may need to recruit minority members.

Mentor programs or *clubs* may also provide needed support for students of color. Successful minority graduates of your high school could be used as role models, and successful people of color from the local community can provide inspiration through career day presentations.

Participation of students of color in *extracurricular activities* should be encouraged. However, Cardenas and Zamora (1980) caution that the costs of such participation must be examined; students of color are disproportionately poor and this may limit their ability to participate.

Advisors and counselors need to be sensitized to the emotional and academic needs of nonwhite students. Some schools provide *special counseling programs* for their non-Anglo students. For example, the Moore Public Schools district in Oklahoma provides orientation information, career education, placement, research and evaluation services for students of color. Chemical dependency and suicide prevention counseling are also provided specifically for Native-American students (Bennett 1989).

Your school can inform minority students and their parents about options for college, including colleges with special ethnic programs, and you can develop networks to obtain information on current financial aid opportunities or educational programs for students of color (Office of Minority Affairs 1988). One example of a financial aid opportunity and educational program for students of color actually fulfills two goals. A school district in Wisconsin provides monetary and employment incentives for students of color to continue their education after high school, and at the same time attempts to increase the number of minority teachers in the state. Seniors may apply for a stipend if they enroll in a teacher preparation program at a Wisconsin state school (Grohe 1989).

The Urban Summer Education Program is a local two-week summer seminar for black high school students that encourages them to finish high school, attend college, and enter the teaching profession (Matcznski and Ellis 1989). Such encouragement is needed for students of color to picture themselves as educators. The presence of more teachers of color, in turn, inspires other students.

Another means of providing special encouragement for students of color is to form a *liaison* between your school and a local higher education institution. While working with a primarily Navajo school district, researchers from Western New Mexico University were able to delineate potential areas of conflict between Navajo students and public education. This information enables public school personnel to identify and aid high-risk Navajo students (French 1990).

Questions for Self-Evaluation

1. Does my school provide special encouragement for its students of color?
2. Are ideas and participation from teachers of color, parents, and members of the community solicited?

3. Does my school's PTA work with multicultural educational goals in mind?

4. Are PTA members representative of the cultural diversity of my school?

5. Does my school use mentors or role models to encourage students of color?

6. Are students of color encouraged to participate in extracurricular activities?

7. Does my school provide special counseling programs for students of color?

8. Are students of color made aware of financial aid opportunities and college options?

9. Does my school work with local higher education institutions to encourage students of color?

How to Get Started

- Solicit the contributions of teachers of color, parents, and members of the community regarding the kind of instruction they desire for their children.

- Encourage minority involvement with the school through Parent Teacher Associations, mentor programs, and career days.

- Encourage minority students to become involved in extracurricular activities.

- Sensitize advisors and counselors to the emotional and academic needs of students of color and provide special counseling programs and services.

- Form a liaison between your school and a local institution of higher learning.

References

Aaron, R., and G. Powell. (1982). "Feedback Practices as a Function of Teacher and Pupil Race During Reading Group Instruction." *Journal of Negro Education* 51, 1: 55–68.

Adair, A.V. (1984). *Desegregation: The Illusion of Black Progress.* Lanham, Md.: University Press of America.

Adams, D. (1990). "The Deep Meaning of Native American Schooling, 1880–1900." In *Facing Racism in Education*, edited by N. Hidalgo, C.L McDowell, and E.V. Siddle (pp. 162–188). Cambridge, Mass.: Harvard Educational Review.

Apple, M. (1990). *Ideology and Curriculum.* New York: Routledge.

Asante, M. (December 1991/January 1992). "Afrocentric Curriculum." *Educational Leadership* 49, 4: 28–31.

Banks, J.A. (1981). *Multicultural Education.* Boston: Allyn and Bacon.

Banks, J.A. (1991). "Multicultural Education: For Freedom's Sake." *Educational Leadership* 49, 4: 32–36.

Baratz, J. (1986). "Black Participation in the Teacher Pool." Paper prepared for the Task Force on Teaching as a Profession, Carnegie Forum on Education and the Economy.

Bastian, A., N. Fruchter, M. Gittell, C. Greer, and K. Haskins. (1986). *Choosing Equality: The Case for Democratic Schooling.* Philadelphia: Temple University Press.

Bennett, C. (1989). *Secondary Guidance Manual.* Moore, Okla.: Moore Public Schools.

Burgess, B. (1980). "Parenting in the Native-American Community." In *Parenting in a Multicultural Society*, edited by M. Fantini et al. (pp. 78–95). New York: Longman.

Bowles, S., and H. Gintis. (1976). *Schooling in Capitalist America.* New York: Basic Books.

Cardenas, J., and G. Zamora. (1980). "The Early Education of Minority Children." In *Parenting in a Multicultural Society*, edited by M. Fantini et al. (pp. 101–132). New York: Longman.

Carnegie Task Force on Teaching as a Profession. (1986). *A Nation Prepared: Teachers for the 21st Century.* New York: Carnegie Forum on Education and the Economy.

Cazden, C.B. (1988). *Classroom Discourse.* Portsmouth, N.H.: Heinemann.

Charles, J. (1991). "Celebrating the Diversity of American Indian Literature." *The Alan Review* 18, 3: 4–8.

Cummins, J. (1990). "Empowering Minority Students: A Framework for Intervention." In *Facing Racism in Education*, edited by N.M. Hidalgo et al. (pp. 50–68). Cambridge Mass.: Harvard Educational Review.

Darling-Hammond, L., and K.J. Pittman. (1987). "Career Choices for Minorities: Who Will Teach?" Paper prepared for the National Education Association and Council of Chief State School Officers Task Force on Minorities in Teaching.

Davis, S. (1986). "The Participation of Indian and Metis Parents in the School System." *Canadian Journal of Native Education* 13, 2: 32–39.

Delpit, L. (1990). "The Silenced Dialogue: Power and Pedagogy in Educating Other People's Children." In *Facing Racism in Education*, edited by N. Hidalgo et al. (pp. 84–102). Cambridge, Mass.: Harvard Educational Review.

DeWitt, K. (September 13, 1991). "Large Increase is Predicted in Minorities in U.S. Schools." *The New York Times National*, p. A14.

Donato, R., M. Menchaca, and R. Valencia. (1991). "Segregation, Desegregation, and Integration of Chicano Students: Problems and Prospects." In *Chicano School Failure and Success*, edited by R. Valencia (pp. 27–63). New York: Falmer Press.

Farrell, K.J. (1990). "On the Growing Shortage of Black and Hispanic Teachers." *English Journal* 79, 1: 39–46.

Fiske, E.B. (1991). *Smart Schools, Smart Kids*. New York: Simon & Schuster.

Flores, H. (December 1991/January 1992). "Please Do Bother Them." *Educational Leadership* 49, 4: 58–59.

Fordham, S. (1990). "Racelessness as a Factor in Black Students' School Success: Pragmatic Strategy or Pyrrhic Victory." In *Facing Racism in Education*, edited by N.M. Hidalgo et al. (pp. 232–262). Cambridge, Mass.: Harvard Educational Review.

Fordham, S., and J. Ogbu. (1986). "Black Students' School Success: Coping with the 'Burden of Acting White.'" *The Urban Review* 18: 176–206.

French, L. (1990). *Assessing American Indian Needs in New Mexico*. Gallup, N.M.: Western New Mexico University Evaluative Report.

Futrell, M.H., and S.P. Robinson. (1986). "Testing Teachers: An Overview of NEA's Position, Policy and Involvement." *Journal of Negro Education* 55: 397–404.

Gay, G. (1990). "Achieving Educational Equality Through Curriculum Desegregation." *Phi Delta Kappan* 72, 1: 56–62.

Giroux, H. (1988). *Teachers as Intellectuals*. New York: Bergin & Garvey Publ.

Gougis, R.A. (1986). "The Effects of Prejudice and Stress on the Academic Performance of Black Americans." In *The School Achievement of Minority Children*, edited by U. Neisser (pp. 145–158). Hillsdale, N.J.: Lawrence Erlbaum Associates.

Graham, P.A. (1987). "Black Teachers: A Drastically Scarce Resource." *Phi Delta Kappan* 68, 8: 598–605.

Greer, C. (1972). *The Great School Legend*. New York: Basic Books.

Grohe, B. (1989). "Today's Top Minority Students Will Teach for Us Tomorrow." *Executive Educator* 11, 2: 21.

Haberman, M. (1989). "More Minority Teachers." *Phi Delta Kappan* 70: 771–776.

Hale-Benson, J.E. (1986). *Black Children: Their Roots, Culture and Learning Styles*. Baltimore: The Johns Hopkins University Press.

Hernandez, H. (1989). *Multicultural Education*. Columbus: Merrill Publishing Company.

Hidalgo, N.M., C.L. McDowell, and E.V. Siddle, eds. (1990). *Facing Racism in Education*. Cambridge, Mass.: Harvard Educational Review.

Hilliard, A.G., III, L. Payton-Stewart, and L.O. Williams, eds. (1990). *Infusion of African and African American Content in the School Curriculum*. Morristown, N.J.: Aaron Press.

Irvine, J.J. (1988). "An Analysis of the Problem of Disappearing Black Educators." *Elementary School Journal* 88: 503–513.

Jackson, G., and C. Cosca. (1974). "The Inequality of Educational Opportunity in the Southwest: An Observational Study of Ethnically Mixed Classrooms." *American Educational Research Journal* 11: 219–229.

Jor'dan, J. (1990). "How PTAs Can Celebrate Differences." *PTA Today* 15, 3: 19–21.

Kagan, S. (1977). "Social Motives and Behaviors of Mexican-American and Anglo-American Children." In *Chicano Psychology*, edited by J. Martinez. (pp. 45–86). New York: Academic Press.

Kagan, S. (December 1990/January 1991). "On Cooperative Learning, A Conversation with Spencer Kagan." *Educational Leadership* 47, 4: 8–11.

Kaestle, C.F. (1983). *Pillars of the Republic*. New York: Hill and Wang.

Katz, M.B. (1975). *Class Bureaucracy and Schools: The Illusion of Educational Change in America*. New York: Praeger.

Koerner, J. (February 1992). "The Best of Both Worlds." *The Colorado College Bulletin*.

Kozol, J. (1985). *Illiterate America*. Garden City, N.Y.: Anchor Press/Doubleday.

Kreitzer, A., G. Madaus, and W. Haney. (1989). "Competency Testing and Dropouts." In *Dropouts from School Issues,*

Dilemmas, and Solutions, edited by L. Weis et al. (pp. 129–152). Albany: State University of New York Press.

Lake, E. (1990). "An Indian Father's Plea." *Teacher* 2, 1: 49–52.

Linn, R., G. Madaus, and J. Pedulla. (1982). "Minimum Competency Testing: Cautions on the State of the Art." *American Journal of Education* 91: 1–35.

Locust, C. (1990). "Wounding the Spirit: Discrimination and Traditional American Indian Belief Systems." In *Facing Racism in Education*, edited by N. Hidalgo et al. (pp. 103–117). Cambridge, Mass.: Harvard Educational Review.

Lynch, J. (1987). *Prejudice Reduction and the Schools*. New York: Nichols Publishing.

MacLeod, J. (1987). *Ain't No Makin' It*. Boulder, Col.: Westview Press.

Mann, D. (1989). "Can We Help Dropouts? Thinking About the Undoable." In *Dropouts from School: Issues, Dilemmas, and Solutions*, edited by L. Weis, E. Farrar, and H. Petrie. (pp. 67–80). Albany: State University of New York Press.

Martinez, J., ed. (1977). *Chicano Psychology*. New York: Academic Press.

Matcznski, T., and J. Ellis. (1989). "A Proposal to Counter Lack of Activity." *Action in Teacher Education* 11, 2: 42–46.

Mercer, J. (1977). "Identifying the Gifted Chicano Child." In *Chicano Psychology*, edited by J. Martinez. (pp. 155–173). New York: Academic Press.

Miller-Jones, D. (1989). "Culture and Testing." *American Psychologist* 8: 360–366.

Molnar, A. (October 1989). "Racism in America: A Continuing Dilemma." *Educational Leadership* 47, 2: 71–72.

Murray, C.B., and R.M. Clark. (1990). "Targets of Racism." *American School Board Journal* 177, 6: 22–24.

New York State Social Studies Review and Development Committee. (1991). *One Nation, Many Peoples: A Declaration of Cultural Interdependence*. New York.

Nobles, W. (1990). "The Infusion of African and African-American Content: A Question of Content and Intent." In *Infusion of African American Content in the School Curriculum*, edited by A. Hilliard et al. (pp. 5–26). Morristown, N.J.: Aaron Press.

Oakes, J. (1986a). "Keeping Track, Part 1: The Policy and Practice of Curriculum Inequality." *Phi Delta Kappan* 68, 1: 12–18.

Oakes, J. (1986b). "Keeping Track, Part 2: Curriculum Inequality and School Reform." *Phi Delta Kappan* 68, 2: 148–154.

Oakes, J. (1988). "Tracking in Mathematics and Science Education: A Structural Contribution to Unequal Schooling." In *Class, Race and Gender in American Education*, edited by L. Weis. (pp. 106–125). Albany: State University of New York Press.

Office of Minority Affairs. (1988). *Multicultural Assessment Plan.* Boston: National Association of Independent Schools.

Ogbu, J.U. (1986). "The Consequences of the American Caste System." In *The School Achievement of Minority Children,* edited by U. Neisser. (pp. 19–56). Hillsdale, N.J.: Lawrence Erlbaum Associates.

Ogbu, J.U. (1988). "Class Stratification, Racial Stratification, and Schooling." In *Class, Race and Gender in American Education,* edited by L. Weis. (pp. 163–182). Albany: State University of New York Press.

Ortiz, F.I. (1988). "Hispanic-American Children's Experiences in Classrooms: A Comparison Between Hispanic and Non-Hispanic Children." In *Class, Race and Gender in American Education,* edited by L. Weis. (pp. 63–86). Albany: State University of New York Press.

Pang, V.O. (1990). "Ethnic Prejudice: Still Alive and Hurtful." In *Facing Racism in Education,* edited by N.M. Hidalgo et al. (pp. 28–32). Cambridge, Mass.: Harvard Educational Review.

Payne, C. (1989). "Urban Teachers and Dropout-Prone Students: The Uneasy Partners." In *Dropouts from School: Issues, Dilemmas, and Solutions,* edited by L. Weis et al. (pp. 113–128). Albany: State University of New York Press.

Pearl, A. (1991). "Systematic and Institutional Factors in Chicano School Failure." In *Chicano School Failure and Success,* edited by R. Valencia. (pp. 273–320). New York: Falmer Press.

Philips, S. (1983). *The Invisible Culture: Communication in the Classroom and Community on the Warm Springs Indian Reservation.* White Plains, N.Y.: Longman.

Pine, G., and A. Hilliard. (1990). "Rx for Racism: Imperatives for America's Schools." *Phi Delta Kappan* 71, 8: 593–600.

Pollard, D.S. (October 1989). "Reducing the Impact of Racism on Students." *Educational Leadership* 47, 2: 73–75.

Quality Education for Minorities Project. (1990). *Education That Works: An Action Plan for the Education of Minorities.* Cambridge, Mass.: Quality Education for Minorities Project.

Ramirez, M., and B. Cox. (1980). "Parenting for Multiculturalism: a Mexican-American Model." In *Parenting in a Multicultural Society,* edited by M. Fantini et al. (pp. 151–178). New York: Longman.

Reinhold, R. (September 29, 1991). "Class Struggle." *New York Times Magazine.* pp. 26–52.

Rueda, R. (1991). "An Analysis of Special Education as a Response to the Diminished Academic Achievement of Chicano Students." In *Chicano School Failure and Success,* edited by R. Valencia. (pp. 252–270). New York: Falmer Press.

Rumberger, R. (1991). "Chicano Dropouts: A Review of Research and Policy Issues." In *Chicano School Failure and Success*, edited by R. Valencia. (pp. 64–89). New York: Falmer Press.

Rosenshine, B. (1971). "Teaching Behavior Related to Pupil Achievement: Review of Research." In *Research into Classroom Process: Recent Developments and Next Steps*, edited by I. Westbury et al. (pp. 51–98). New York: Teachers College Press.

Sagar, H., and J. Schofield. (1984). "Integrating the Desegregated School: Problems and Possibilities." In *Advances in Motivation and Achievement; The Effects of School Desegregation on Motivation and Achievement*, edited by D.E. Bartz and M. Maehr (pp. 203–242). Greenwich, Conn.: JAI Press.

Schierbeck, H.M. (1981). "Confronting the Continuing Dilemma." *Integrateducation* 19, 1–2: 2–6.

Selakovich, D. (1984). *Schooling in America*. New York: Longman Inc.

Shor, I. (1986). *Culture Wars*. Boston: Routledge & Kegan Paul.

Sleeter, C., and C. Grant. (1990). "An Analysis of Multicultural Education in the United States." In *Facing Racism in Education*, edited by N.M. Hidalgo et al. (pp. 138–161). Cambridge, Mass.: Harvard Educational Review.

Sleeter, C. (1991). *Empowerment Through Multicultural Education*. Albany, N.Y.: S.U.N.Y. Press.

Snyderman, M., and S. Rothman. (1987). "Survey of Expert Opinion on Intelligence and Aptitude Testing." *American Psychologist* 42: 137–144.

Solomon, R.P. (1989). "Dropping Out of Academics: Black Youth and the Sports Subculture in a Cross-National Perspective." In *Dropouts from School Issues, Dilemmas, and Solutions*, edited by L. Weis et al. (pp. 79–96). Albany: State University of New York Press.

Stanlaw, J., and A. Peshkin. (1988). "Black Visibility in a Multi-Ethnic High School." In *Class, Race and Gender in American Education*, edited by L. Weis. (pp. 209–229). Albany: State University of New York Press.

Stewart, J. (1989). "In Quest of Role Models: Change in Black Teacher Representation in Urban School Districts, 1968–1986." *Journal of Negro Education* 58: 140–152.

Stover, D. (1990). "The New Racism." *American School Board Journal* 177, 6: 14–18.

Stover, L. (1991). "Exploring and Celebrating Cultural Diversity and Similarity Through Young Adult Novels." *The Alan Review* 18, 3: 12–15.

Tyack, D.B. (1974). *The One Best System*. Cambridge, Mass.: Harvard University Press.

Thomas G.E. (1987). "Black Students in U.S. Graduate and Professional Schools in the 1980's: A National and Institutional Assessment." *Harvard Educational Review* 57: 261–282.

U.S. Commission on Civil Rights. (1973). *Mexican American Education Study, Report 5: Teachers and Students; Differences in Teacher Interaction with Mexican American and Anglo Students.* Washington, D.C.: Government Printing Office.

U.S. Commission on Civil Rights. (1976). *Fulfilling the Letter and Spirit of the Law: Desegregation of the Nation's Schools.* Washington, D.C.: Government Printing Office.

Valencia, R., ed. (1991). *Chicano School Failure and Success.* New York: Falmer Press.

Valencia, R., and S. Aburto. (1991). "The Uses and Abuses of Educational Testing: Chicanos as a Case in Point." In *Chicano School Failure and Success,* edited by R. Valencia. (pp. 203–251). New York: Falmer Press.

Wehlage, G., and R. Rutter. (1987). "Dropping Out: How Much Do Schools Contribute to the Problem?" In *School Dropouts: Patterns and Policies,* edited by G. Natriello. (pp. 29–46). New York: Teachers College Press.

Wehlage, G. (1989). "Dropping Out: Can Schools Be Expected to Prevent It?" In *Dropouts from School: Issues, Dilemmas, and Solutions,* edited by L. Weiss et al. (pp. 1–22). Albany: State University of New York Press.

Weis, L. (1985). *Between Two Worlds: Black Students in an Urban Community College.* Boston: Routledge and Kegan Paul.

Weis, L., ed. (1988). *Class, Race and Gender in American Education.* Albany: State University of New York Press.